The Unexplained

by **Michael Burgan**

Consultant:
Curt Nelson
Researcher
Bigfoot Field Researchers Organization

Capstone
press

Mankato, Minnesota

Edge Books are published by Capstone Press
151 Good Counsel Drive, P.O. Box 669, Mankato, Minnesota 56002
www.capstonepress.com

Library of Congress Cataloging-in-Publication Data
Burgan, Michael.
    Bigfoot / by Michael Burgan.
        p. cm.—(Edge books. The unexplained)
    Includes bibliographical references and index.
    Contents: The Legend of Bigfoot—History of Bigfoot—Searching for Bigfoot—
Looking for answers.
    ISBN 0-7368-2715-3 (hardcover)
    1. Sasquatch—Juvenile literature. [1. Sasquatch.] I. Title. II. Series.
QL89 .2.S2B87 2005
001.944—dc22   2003024297

Editorial Credits

Carrie A. Braulick, editor; Juliette Peters, designer; Kelly Garvin, photo researcher;
    Eric Kudalis, product planning editor

Photo Credits

AP/Wide World Photos/Lloyd Young, 21
Corbis/Reuters NewMedia Inc., 19
Fortean Picture Library, 7, 29; Christopher L. Murphy, cover; Cliff Crook, 12, 15, 23;
    René Dahinden, 5, 6, 11, 17; William M. Rebsamen, 26
Illustration by Alicia Bateman, 27
Kathy Moskowitz, 9
Mary Evans Picture Library, 25
Richard Noll 2003, 20

1 2 3 4 5 6 09 08 07 06 05 04

Table of Contents

FEATURES

Chapter 1

The Legend of Bigfoot

In 1967, Roger Patterson and Bob Gimlin rode horses through the mountains of northern California. Across a stream, they spotted a tall hairy figure. The creature walked on two legs. It was more than 6 feet (1.8 meters) tall. Hair covered its body.

The horses became frightened. Patterson lost his balance and fell off his horse. He grabbed his movie camera before he hit the ground. Patterson filmed the animal as he ran toward it. Gimlin stayed behind. He held a rifle in case the animal attacked. Patterson's camera then ran out of film. The beast walked into the woods.

Learn about:
- Roger Patterson and Bob Gimlin
- Location of sightings
- Bigfoot descriptions

Patterson and Gimlin's film shows a large hairy creature walking on two legs.

EDGE FACT

▲ Patterson and Gimlin said the Bigfoot walked toward the woods before they lost sight of it.

Patterson and Gimlin said they had made the first film of a Bigfoot. The film caused more people to become interested in Bigfoots.

About Bigfoot

North Americans have reported thousands of Bigfoot sightings. People living in the northwestern United States and Canada report the most Bigfoot sightings. People living in other countries also say they have seen Bigfoots. Scientists do not know for certain whether the creatures exist.

People have reported Bigfoots as far south ▼ as Florida.

Chapter 2

History of Bigfoot

For thousands of years, people have told stories about wild hairy beasts that look like humans. Some stories could be based on Bigfoot sightings.

American Indians may have been the first people in North America to see a Bigfoot. Some tribes in Canada called it *sésqec*, or "wild man of the woods." In English, the name became Sasquatch.

Learn about:
• American Indian reports
• Albert Ostman
• Jerry Crew's discovery

American Indian paintings
show large creatures
that look like Bigfoots.

Early Reports

In 1784, a newspaper in London, England, published one of the first articles about a North American Bigfoot. The story said American Indians in Canada had captured a large furry animal that looked like a human.

Bigfoot reports continued in the 1800s. In 1818, a newspaper reported that a large humanlike creature had been spotted in the state of New York. Several people looked for the animal. It was never found. In the late 1830s, people reported seeing small hairy humanlike creatures in Pennsylvania and Indiana. Some people thought the creatures were young Bigfoots.

In the 1850s, gold miners in California reported seeing Bigfoots. The men said the Bigfoots sometimes picked up and smashed their mining equipment.

In 1924, Albert Ostman was working as a logger in British Columbia, Canada. He said a Bigfoot kidnapped him. The animal took Ostman to where it lived. Three more Bigfoots were there. Ostman said one of the Bigfoots was at least 8 feet (2.4 meters) tall.

The Chapman family from British Columbia claimed to see a Bigfoot in 1941. The Chapmans said they saw the Bigfoot outside their home near Ruby Creek. It stood about 7 feet (2.1 meters) tall. The Bigfoot took food from a small building near the home. For the next week, the Chapmans saw large footprints near their house.

▲ The Chapmans said they saw a Bigfoot near their home in British Columbia, Canada.

EDGE FACT

A restaurant in Willow Creek, California, sells a Bigfoot hamburger in the shape of a foot.

▲ In 1995, a forest patrol officer said he took this photo of a Bigfoot. Most researchers believe it is fake.

More Cases

Interest in Bigfoots grew after 1958. That year, Jerry Crew was building a road with other workers near Willow Creek, California. He discovered a giant footprint. It was about 2.4 feet (.7 meter) long and 7 inches (18 centimeters) wide. The workers continued seeing large footprints for several days.

Crew made a plaster cast of one of the footprints. Researchers thought the print came from a Bigfoot. Soon, other people began finding large footprints in nearby states.

In the 1960s and 1970s, the number of Bigfoot sightings increased. People went into the woods looking for Bigfoots. Until this time, most people reported seeing the beasts while hiking or doing other outdoor activities.

Reports continued during the 1990s. In 1995, a forest patrol officer said he saw a Bigfoot near Mount Rainier in Washington. He took several photos of the creature.

Chapter 3

Searching for Bigfoot

People formed groups to study Bigfoots as reports increased. In 1995, scientists formed the Bigfoot Field Researchers Organization (BFRO). This group keeps track of Bigfoot sightings and studies Bigfoot evidence. It is the largest group in the world that studies Bigfoots.

Tracking Bigfoots

Researchers carry supplies to help them find Bigfoots. They carry food they think Bigfoots might eat. Some researchers wear goggles that help them see in the dark. Scientists believe the creatures are most active after dark. Researchers also bring cameras designed to work well in the dark.

Learn about:
- Bigfoot researchers
- Search supplies
- Bigfoot footprints

Researchers study footprints they think may be from a Bigfoot.

The BFRO has researched many reports of Bigfoot sightings in Del Norte County in northern California. The county has more Bigfoot sightings than any place in the world. About 24 sightings have been reported in the county. In September 2003, a man said he saw a Bigfoot near a highway in Del Norte county. The next day, another man reported seeing a Bigfoot in the same area.

Footprint Research

Bigfoot researcher Jeff Meldrum is an expert on human and ape feet. Meldrum has studied several casts of footprints people say are from Bigfoots. He believes the details on some prints show that they are real. The footprints are similar to those a human would leave. But the prints have no foot arch. The large size of the prints also shows they were not made by humans. Most of the footprints are at least 14 inches (36 centimeters) long and 6 inches (15 centimeters) wide.

Jimmy Chilcutt studies human fingerprints and footprints at a police department. He has studied about 100 footprint casts people say are from Bigfoots. Chilcutt also studies monkey and ape prints. Chilcutt said at least five casts he studied were from a Bigfoot.

▼ A Bigfoot cast is much larger than a human foot.

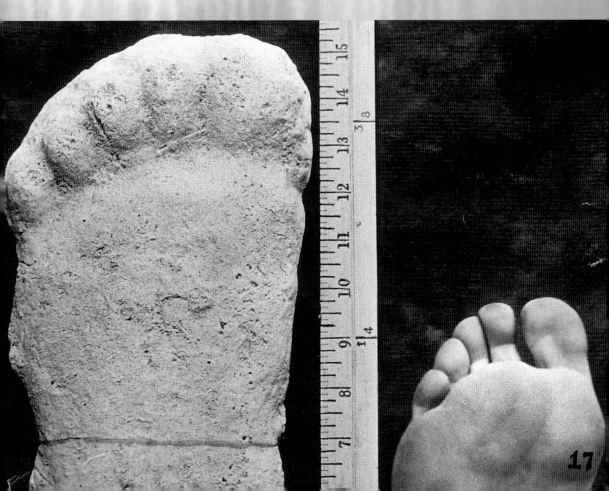

Researchers

Loren Coleman searches for animals that have not been discovered yet. He has studied Bigfoot and other animal mysteries. Coleman studied several famous Bigfoot reports. He wrote a book about them. Coleman believes Bigfoot is a type of ape.

Bigfoot researcher Grover Krantz studied Bigfoot for nearly 40 years. Like Coleman, Krantz believed Bigfoot was a type of ape.

Jane Goodall is known for her studies on chimpanzees. Goodall believes Bigfoots are real. She has studied the similarities among Bigfoot reports.

Peter Byrne has led many searches for Bigfoots. In the mid-1990s, Byrne ran the Bigfoot Research Project. Members of the project searched for Bigfoots. They studied reports in the northwestern United States. The members also answered a phone hotline. People could call the hotline to report Bigfoot sightings.

EDGE FACT

Several movies have been made about Bigfoots. They include *Harry and the Hendersons* and *The Legend of Boggy Creek*.

⬆ Jane Goodall is well known for her studies on chimpanzees.

Field Trips

Researchers continue to search for Bigfoots. The BFRO organizes field trips each year. In May 2001, BFRO researchers went to southeastern Oklahoma. In 2003, researchers went to Wisconsin and the Chuska Mountains in New Mexico.

The Skookum Cast

In 2000, Bigfoot researchers investigated Gifford Pinchot National Forest in Washington. They placed fruit at several places to attract a Bigfoot. After five days, the researchers checked the fruit locations. At one of the places, they saw an indentation in the mud. The indentation was in the shape of a large animal. It looked like the animal was lying on its side when it reached out to grab fruit. The researchers made a plaster cast from the indentation. The cast shows part of a leg and arm.

The 400-pound (181-kilogram) cast is called the Skookum Cast. The researchers found the indentation in an area known as Skookum Meadows. Some scientists believe the cast is from a Bigfoot.

During field trips, researchers look for signs of Bigfoots. They search for Bigfoot tracks and hair. They also look for dens or other shelters where Bigfoots may live.

In 1998, Bigfoot researchers found hair in California that may be from a Bigfoot.

21

Chapter 4

Looking for Answers

People have different theories to explain Bigfoots. Some of these ideas are based on scientific evidence. Other theories are guesses. Researchers study all evidence before they decide to believe a theory.

Some people believe Bigfoots are bears. Large bears leave footprints almost as large as the prints people say Bigfoots left. Bears also can stand on two feet. Bigfoot experts agree that some people who see bears mistake them for Bigfoots.

Learn about:
• Hoaxes
• Gigantos
• Neanderthals

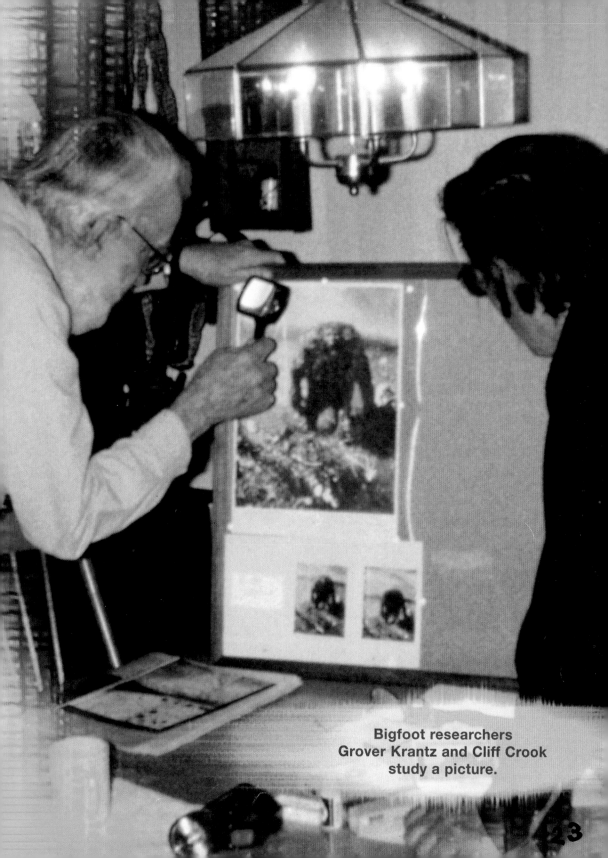

Bigfoot researchers
Grover Krantz and Cliff Crook
study a picture.

23

In 2002, researchers learned that the first famous Bigfoot footprints might have been a hoax. Jerry Crew had worked for a man named Ray Wallace. When Wallace died, his family said that he had created the footprints from 1958. They said he had wanted to fool people. But some researchers still believe the footprints were real.

Neanderthals

Some people think Bigfoots are related to humans. Neanderthals were early relatives of humans. They lived more than 30,000 years ago.

Some researchers think a few Neanderthals might have survived. They believe the Neanderthals changed over thousands of years. They eventually became today's Bigfoots.

▲ Neanderthals were relatives of humans.

Giant Apes

In recent years, some scientists have suggested another theory to explain Bigfoots. They think the creatures are relatives of giant apes called gigantos. Gigantos lived in Asia about 400,000 years ago.

The scientists think a few gigantos survived. They believe they came to North America thousands of years ago. At that time, land bridges connected Asia to North America.

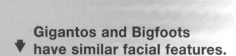

Gigantos and Bigfoots have similar facial features.

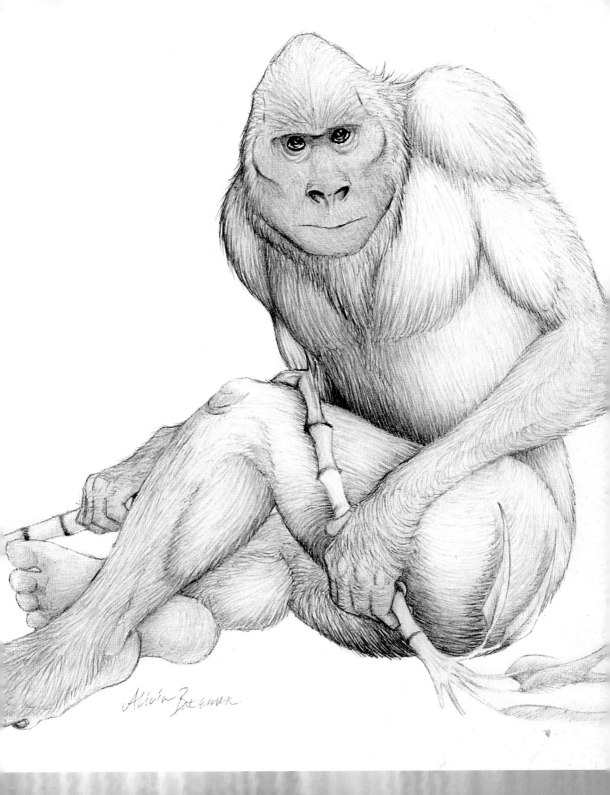

▲ Gigantos lived in Asia more than 400,000 years ago.

Searching for More Proof

Some scientists do not believe Bigfoots exist. Some of these scientists say Bigfoot is not real because no one has found the body or bones of a dead Bigfoot. Other scientists say the reason for the lack of bones is because few Bigfoots exist. They believe Bigfoots live and die in areas far from people's normal living areas. After Bigfoots die, other animals eat their bodies. The bones and other remaining pieces break down.

Researchers still hunt for proof that Bigfoots exist. They may not be sure what they are or how they got to North America. Yet researchers hope to someday solve the mystery of the large humanlike beasts.

Is Patterson's Film Real?

Some people say Patterson's film from 1967 is a fake. They think the figure is a person dressed in an ape suit. Scientists at the North American Science Institute studied the film. They said the creature moved like an animal. They also said its arms were too long to be a person's arms.

Movie producers in Los Angeles, California, also said Patterson's film is of a person in an ape suit. They said the suit was made by John Chambers. Chambers is a famous movie costume designer. In 1997, Chambers said he did not make the suit.

Roger Patterson holds casts he made of footprints he found after filming the creature. ➡

29

Glossary

cast (KAST)—a model of an object in plaster; casts show details of the original object.

evidence (EV-uh-duhnss)—information that helps prove something is true or false

hoax (HOHKS)—a trick to make people believe something that is not true

Neanderthal (nee-AN-dur-thal)—an early type of human who lived more than 30,000 years ago

plaster (PLASS-tur)—a pasty substance made of lime, sand, and water; plaster hardens over time.

theory (THEE-ur-ee)—an idea that explains something that is unknown

Read More

Coleman, Loren, and Patrick Huyghe. *The Field Guide to Bigfoot, Yeti, and Other Mystery Primates Worldwide.* New York: Avon Books, 1999.

Cox, Greg. *Bigfoot.* Unsolved Mysteries. New York: Rosen, 2002.

Innes, Brian. *Giant Humanlike Beasts.* Unsolved Mysteries. Austin, Texas: Raintree Steck-Vaughn, 1999.

Internet Sites

FactHound offers a safe, fun way to find Internet sites related to this book. All of the sites on FactHound have been researched by our staff.

Here's how:

1. Visit *www.facthound.com*
2. Type in this special code **0736827153** for age-appropriate sites. Or enter a search word related to this book for a more general search.
3. Click on the **Fetch It** button.

FactHound will fetch the best sites for you!

Index